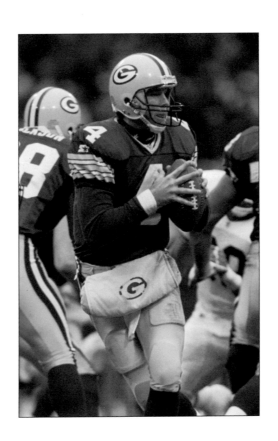

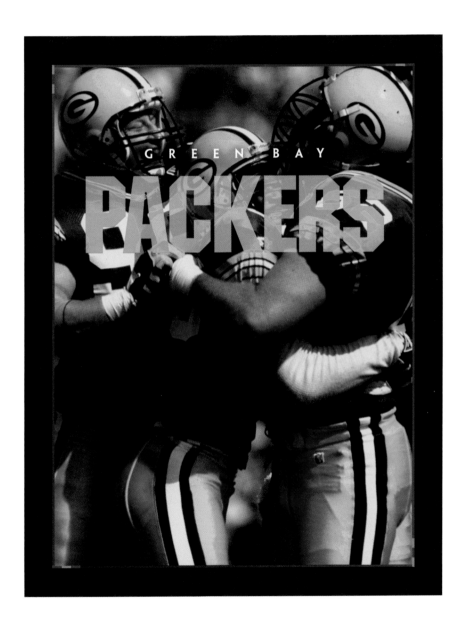

GREEN BAY
PACKERS

MICHAEL GOODMAN

CREATIVE ✿ EDUCATION

Published by Creative Education
123 South Broad Street, Mankato, Minnesota 56001
Creative Education is an imprint of The Creative Company

Designed by Rita Marshall
Cover illustration by Rob Day

Photos by: Allsport Photography, Associated Press, Bettmann Archive,
Duomo, Focus on Sports, Fotosport, and SportsChrome.

Library of Congress Cataloging-in-Publication Data

Goodman, Michael E.
Green Bay Packers/ by Michael Goodman.
p. cm. — (NFL Today)
Summary: Traces the history of the team from its beginnings through 1996.
ISBN 0-88682-793-0

1. Green Bay Packers (Football team)—History—Juvenile literature.
[1. Green Bay Packers (Football team) 2. Football—History.]
I. Title. II. Series.

GV956.G7G66   1996   96-15236
796.332'64'0977563—dc20

123456

A long the western shores of Lake Michigan, in the north-eastern section of Wisconsin, is a land of rushing rivers, pine forests and abundant wildlife. In the 1630s, a French explorer and fur trader named Jean Nicolet first explored the area, searching for a trade route from the Great Lakes to the Mississippi River. Nicolet never found that route, but he did establish a frontier post along an inlet called Green Bay. It grew into a thriving community that today is noted for its rustic beauty, tasty cheeses and world famous professional football team—the Green Bay Packers.

Pro football has been an important part of life in Green Bay

Don Hutson (#14) with Curly Lambeau and Irv Comp.

since 1919. The Packers, one of the oldest franchises in the National Football League, have a long and exciting history. They are the first and only NFL team to win three consecutive league titles, and they've done it twice. They were the first Super Bowl champs, winning Super Bowls I and II under legendary coach Vince Lombardi. They were also the club that revolutionized pro football by making the passing game an integral part of the offensive attack.

Packer greats over the years—like Curly Lambeau, Don Hutson, Bart Starr, Ray Nitschke, Paul Hornung, Willie Davis, Sterling Sharpe, Reggie White and Brett Favre—have made their impact on pro football. They have also created a Packer tradition of excellence that has thrilled fans for more than 75 years.

Starting at the top: The Packers posted a 10-1 record in their first season.

THE EARLY YEARS

Professional football began with some strange names for teams and players. It was a time for players with nicknames like "Bronko" and "the Antelope." In 1919, Earl "Curly" Lambeau, one of those pro football pioneers, worked for a meatpacking company in Green Bay. He asked his boss at the Indian Packing Company to put up the $500 needed for equipment and uniforms for a new team. The boss agreed, and Lambeau named the team the "Packers" in gratitude.

The equipment was simple in those early days, and players had to be tough and dedicated. They wore leather helmets without face guards and few, if any, pads. Most played both offense and defense since the team roster was usually less than 20 men. Salaries were even more modest than the equipment. At the end of the Packers' first season, the players split the profits evenly—$16.75 per man.

Quarterback Bart Starr became the leader in the 1960s (page 7).

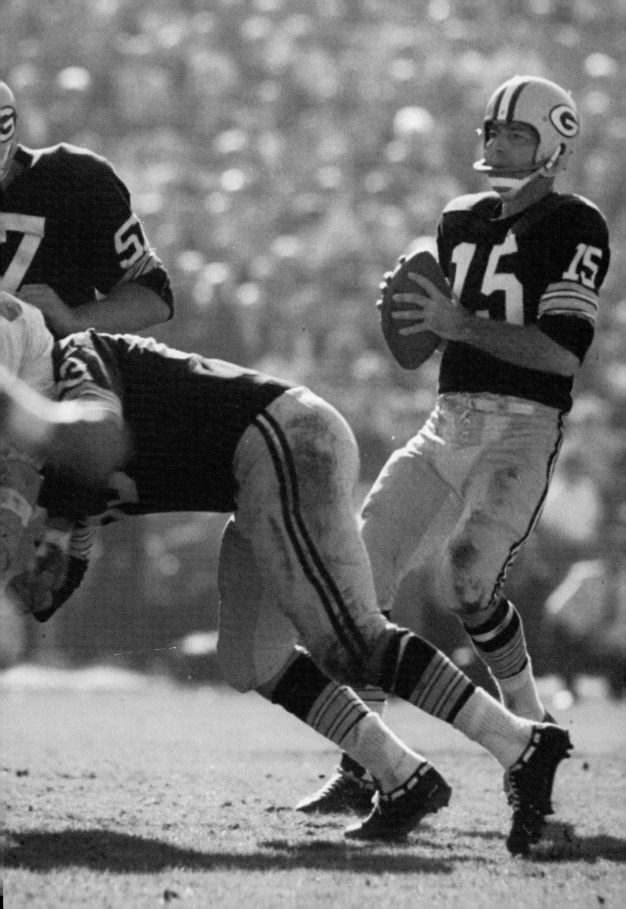

1 9 3 4

Three in a row: Fullback Clarke Hinkle led the Packers in rushing for the third straight season.

Lambeau was a strict disciplinarian who knew how to win. His club responded by going 10-1 in 1919. Lambeau played quarterback and directed the offense. During one early game, three Green Bay running backs were carried from the field with broken bones. Out of necessity, Lambeau began calling passing plays, and the Packers won, 33-0. "That's when I learned the value of the forward pass," he recalled. Lambeau quarterbacked the team for 10 seasons. Then, in 1929, he retired to concentrate solely on coaching the Packers for the next 20 years.

The early Packers, with their combined land and air attack, soon became a powerhouse in the new National Football League and were champions in 1929, 1930 and 1931 with a combined record of 34-5-2. The team's stars included four future Hall of Famers—linemen Cal Hubbard and Mike Michalske and backs Johnny Blood and Clarke Hinkle.

But the best was yet to come. In 1935, a perfect marriage occurred in Green Bay when a young pass receiver from Pine Bluff, Arkansas, named Don Hutson joined the Packers and helped Curly Lambeau turn the passing game into an art form. With his speed and grace, Hutson soon earned the nickname "the Arkansas Antelope."

Hutson made his mark in the league right away. In his first play from scrimmage, he grabbed an 83-yard touchdown strike from quarterback Arnie Herber. It was the first of 488 catches Hutson would make and the first of 99 touchdowns he would score in his record-breaking career.

Hutson's standard of 99 touchdown pass receptions went unchallenged for 44 years, until Seattle's Steve Largent surpassed it in 1989. Several of Hutson's other benchmarks still stand today: most seasons leading the league in touchdown catches (nine), most seasons leading the league in pass receptions (eight) and most consecutive years leading the league in pass catches (five). Hutson was the terror of the NFL and the force behind the Packers' next three league championships in 1936, 1939 and 1944.

When Hutson retired after the 1945 season and Lambeau called it quits in 1949, the first great football era in Green Bay ended, and it would be more than a decade before the club became a winner again. The team really hit rock bottom during the 1958 season, finishing with a 1-10-1 record, the worst in franchise history. It was time for a change.

Rookie coach Vince Lombardi would post a 98-30-4 record over the next nine years.

"COACH"

The biggest change was the addition of a new head coach, Vince Lombardi, a 45-year-old former assistant with the New York Giants. Lombardi was called "Coach" by most people who knew him because he was such a great motivator. Lombardi insisted on an unusually long five-year contract with the Packers, promising to create a winner during that period. He did much more than that. During Lombardi's first five years, the Packers not only had winning records each year, they made the playoffs four times and captured the NFL championship twice. Then, in the next four years, Lombardi led the team to three more league titles.

When Lombardi arrived in Green Bay in 1959, he quickly established his commitment to excellence. At the first team meeting, Lombardi told his players, "I have never been on a losing team, gentlemen, and I do not intend to start now!" The players were clearly impressed, and the club rebounded from its

Defensive tackle Reggie White was trouble for opposing runners (pages 10-11).

Star receiver Max McGee led the Packers with fifty-one receptions for 883 yards.

lowly 1-10-1 season in 1958 to post a winning 7-5 record in 1959.

Lombardi was a taskmaster, but he was also able to enjoy a laugh with his players. Max McGee, a star receiver for Green Bay, remembers: "I could make him laugh, and I know he liked me because of it. He'd back himself into an emotional corner, and I would get him out of it. After we won a game 6-3 on two field goals, he was furious. He told us to forget everything he'd taught us, to scrap it all, that we were going back to basics. He reached down and picked up a football and said, with a sarcastic grin all over his face, 'This is a football.' And I said, 'Slow it down a little, coach. You're going too fast.'"

Lombardi ran the team with a strong hand from the sidelines, but he also had a coach on the field, quarterback Bart Starr. Starr had been drafted out of the University of Alabama in the seventeenth round in 1956 and never showed much promise until Lombardi arrived in Green Bay and made him a starter. Starr rewarded Lombardi's faith in him by setting dozens of NFL records before his retirement in 1971. He completed a higher percentage of passes than any prior quarterback in NFL history (57.4%); threw a record 294 consecutive passes without an interception; led the league in passing in 1962, 1964 and 1966; and was the Most Valuable Player in both Super Bowls I and II. In the eight seasons between 1960 and 1967, the Starr-led Packers posted a sizzling 82-24-4 record and captured five NFL championships.

But there were many more heroes during the Lombardi era. The names could fill their own wing in the Pro Football Hall of Fame: running backs Jim Taylor and Paul Hornung, offensive linemen Forrest Gregg and Jim Ringo and defensive standouts Ray Nitschke, Willie Davis, Willie Wood and Herb Adderley. Two other unsung heroes were offensive guards Jerry Kramer and Fred "Fuzzy" Thurston, whose blocks often sprung Green Bay running backs for long gains. Kramer made one of the most remembered blocks in NFL history during a game that is now labeled "the Ice Bowl."

It was December 31, 1967, and the Dallas Cowboys were playing at Green Bay's Lambeau Field for the NFL championship. The temperature was a bitter -13 degrees, and the Cowboys were wearing gloves and frowns. Lombardi told the gloveless Packers, "You've got to be bigger than the weather to be a winner."

Green Bay found themselves in a tough struggle both with the elements and the Cowboys. Late in the game, with the sun disappearing and the temperatures dropping even lower, the Packers had one final chance to overcome a 17-14 Dallas lead. Starting from their own 31-yard line, Green Bay drove the length of the field. On third down, with the ball inside the Dallas one-yard line and only 16 seconds remaining, Lombardi had a big decision to make. Should the Packers go for a winning touchdown and risk the clock running out if they failed, or kick a short field goal to tie the game and force an overtime period?

"I thought of the fans," Lombardi later said. "I couldn't stand to think of them sitting in those cold stands during overtime." He and Starr agreed that the best plan was a quarterback sneak.

Starr described the play: "We had noticed earlier that Jethro Pugh, the Cowboys' tackle on the left side, charged too high on goal-line situations. So we knew a quarterback sneak would work. Jerry Kramer was confident he could block Pugh."

When the pile of bodies was separated, Starr and Kramer were

1 9 6 4

Running back Paul Hornung scored over 100 points for a record third season.

13

Fullback Jim Taylor rushed for 705 yards and helped his team to the Super Bowl.

both across the goal line, and the Packers had won the game and the NFL title 21-17.

But the season was not yet over for the Packers. For the second straight year, they would take on the champion of the American Football League (AFL) in the Super Bowl. A year earlier, Green Bay had won Super Bowl I, 35-10, over the Kansas City Chiefs. Now they would have a chance to defend their title against the Oakland Raiders.

There was added pressure on the Green Bay players during Super Bowl II. Rumors had spread that "Coach" planned to retire following the game. Lombardi gave a stirring pre-game pep talk, and his players responded with an impressive 33-14 win. Forrest Gregg and Jerry Kramer carried Lombardi from the field on their shoulders. "This is the best way to leave a football field," said Lombardi.

The following year Lombardi served as Green Bay general manager only and appointed Phil Bengtson as head coach. He quickly became bored off the field, however, and began looking for a new coaching challenge. A year later, Lombardi took over the Washington Redskins, a team as bad as the Packers had been before he arrived in Green Bay. He was turning that club around, too, when he became very ill with cancer and died. The entire nation mourned the loss of a truly great man, but nowhere was there more grief than in Green Bay.

PEAKS AND VALLEYS

Following Vince Lombardi's retirement, the Packers went through a series of peaks and valleys, making the playoffs only once during the next 14 years and finishing above .500 only three times. There was a lot of turnover of both players and coaches.

Linebacker Ray Nitschke was known for his ferocious pursuit.   15

1 9 7 5

Veteran running back John Brockington rushed for seven touchdowns, providing team leadership.

In an effort to revive the old Packer tradition, the club's owners brought in Bart Starr as head coach in 1975. Starr, like Lombardi, found a team with potential: John Brockington, the 1971 Rookie of the Year, was at running back, and Chester Marcol, the 1972 Rookie of the Year, was a consistently accurate kicker. But, unlike Lombardi, Starr was never able to create a consistent winner in Green Bay.

Starr's greatest success came in developing a recharged Packer passing attack in the early 1980s. With Lynn Dickey as quarterback and James Lofton and John Jefferson as wide receivers, the Packers became an aerial powerhouse. All three players still hold a number of team passing and receiving records. Running back Eddie Lee Ivery rounded out the offense. Unfortunately, the club lacked defensive muscle, often giving up 30 or more points in a game to the opposition.

In 1982, Starr's team finally reached playoff territory. Green Bay posted a 5-3-1 mark in the strike-shortened season and grabbed a postseason berth for the first time in 11 years.

In the Wild Card playoff game, Dickey threw for more than 300 yards to spearhead a 41-16 romp over the St. Louis Cardinals. That set up a playoff confrontation with the Dallas Cowboys for the first time since "the Ice Bowl." This time the Cowboys won, 37-26.

Green Bay fans were expecting great things from the Packers in 1983. What they received was heart-stopping drama. Four games were decided in overtime—an NFL record. Five others were won or lost by four points or less.

Everything came down to the last game against the Chicago Bears. If the Packers won, they would be division champs and make the playoffs for a second straight year. If they lost, their

Receiver James Lofton demonstrated acrobatic skills as a pass catcher.   17

Linebacker Tim Harris was an All-Pro.

season would be over. With only seconds remaining, Green Bay was up 21-20, but Bears kicker Bob Thomas booted a last-second field goal, sealing the Packers' fate and Bart Starr's as well. A few weeks later, he was fired as team coach and replaced by his former teammate Forrest Gregg.

Vince Lombardi had once called Gregg "the finest player I ever coached." Now Packers fans counted on him to return the team to its former glory.

Gregg decided to emphasize defense over offense, bringing in players such as defensive end Alphonso Carreker, linebacker Tim Harris and defensive back Mossy Cade. But the team never became a winner. Following a miserable 5-9-1 campaign in 1987, Gregg resigned to become coach at his alma mater, Southern Methodist University.

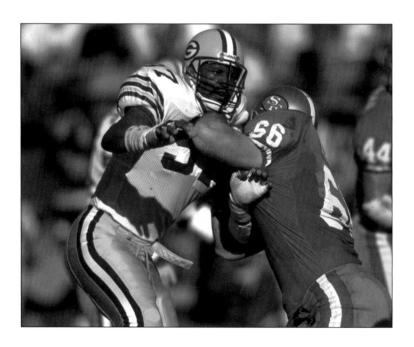

After Gregg's departure, Green Bay management decided to look outside the Packer family for a new head coach. They selected Cleveland Browns offensive coordinator Lindy Infante, who had helped build winners as an assistant for many years in Cleveland and Cincinnati.

1 9 8 9

He's Magic! Quarterback Don Majkowski led the Packers to a string of come-from-behind victories.

The Florida native came to Wisconsin filled with enthusiasm. "I feel good about where we're going," he told fans. "I feel good about the majority of people who are going to get us there."

Infante based much of his optimism on the presence of two unusual talents known as "Majik" and "the Mouth." Majik was quarterback Don Majkowski, a late-round draft pick in 1987 out of the University of Virginia. "The Mouth" was linebacker Tim Harris, a brash and ferocious player drafted by Forrest Gregg in 1986 out of Memphis State. Harris was known both for hard hitting and "trash talking." That's how he earned his nickname. He would break through the opposition line and sack the quarterback. Then he would yell into the quarterback's face: "Gonna be a looonnnnggg day. Wooooooohooooo!" That really annoyed opponents, but Green Bay fans loved Harris' antics and appreciated his talent.

Majkowski surprised most experts by winning the starting berth mid-way through his rookie year. He really came into his own in 1988 after Infante arrived. The new coach encouraged the young quarterback to increase his knowledge of football strategy. "I want you to be a manipulator, not a gunslinger," Infante said. Majkowski listened and began spending a lot more time studying game films.

One thing Infante didn't have to teach Majkowski was the

Sterling Sharpe was the Packers' leading deep receiving threat in 1989.

desire to win. Majkowski's enthusiasm soon rubbed off on his teammates, who began believing in themselves. His ability to scramble behind the line of scrimmage and turn potentially dangerous situations into long gainers also made him a crowd favorite and earned him the nickname "Majik."

Majik performed his greatest tricks during the 1989 season, when his late-game heroics helped Green Bay transform from a 4-12 team in 1988 into a 10-6 contender. Majik and second-year wide receiver Sterling Sharpe became the most potent passing combo in the league. Majik set club records with 599 attempts and 353 completions, and Sharpe led the NFL with 90 catches. Both players earned Pro Bowl berths along with Tim Harris, who topped all NFC defenders with 19.5 sacks.

Green Bay fans were certain that a new "golden age" in Packer history was starting. Unfortunately, injuries to both Majik and Sharpe caused the Pack to fall to 6-10 in 1990 and 4-12 in 1991. Lindy Infante was dismissed, and it was time to start all over again.

Head coach Mike Holmgren led the Packers back to respectability with a 9-7 record.

THE HOLMGREN ERA BEGINS

Step one in the rebuilding effort, of course, meant finding the right coach. The San Francisco 49ers were one of the dominant teams of the 1980s, particularly on offense. That's why Green Bay management recruited 49ers offensive coordinator Mike Holmgren to become the team's new head coach.

Holmgren was noted for his ability to develop young quarterbacks. He had already helped San Francisco's Steve Young become the top-rated passer in NFL history, and he hoped to duplicate this feat with another young signal-caller, Brett Favre,

Left to right: Edgar Bennett, Bryce Paup, Ken Ruettgers, Chris Jacke.

whom the Packers had obtained in a trade from Atlanta before the 1992 season.

Favre had sat on the bench for most of 1991, watching Chris Miller lead the Falcons, and he was thrilled to join Holmgren in Green Bay. Leading a revitalized Packers offense, Favre completed over 300 passes for more than 3,200 yards in 1992. An NFL record 108 of those passes went to Sterling Sharpe, now fully recovered from his injuries. Rookie halfback Edgar Bennett added another dimension to the Packers attack as both a rusher and receiver, while linebackers Tony Bennett and Bryce Paup keyed a greatly improved defense.

1 9 9 5

Cornerback LeRoy Butler led the Packers defense with six interceptions.

The team's new stars helped the Packers win six of their last seven games to finish at 9-7. Green Bay would have made the playoffs but for a loss in the final game of the season against Minnesota.

The next year, the Pack was truly back. Favre and Sharpe combined for 112 passes, surpassing their own NFL record. Green Bay also added another major weapon, future Hall of Fame defensive end Reggie White, who signed as a free agent before the 1993 season. White, the NFL's career quarterback sack leader, keyed a defense that gave up more than 30 points only twice all year. "I don't think there has ever been a guy at his position with Reggie White's combination of size, speed and strength," said one opposition coach.

Green Bay finished at 9-7 for the second straight year, its first back-to-back winning seasons since the Super Bowl teams of 1966 and 1967. They also made the playoffs for the first time since 1982. But the Packers weren't ready to stop there.

In the Wild Card contest against the Detroit Lions, Favre led the Pack on an exciting last-minute drive. With 55 seconds to

Defensive end Sean Jones excelled against the run (pages 26-27).

Robert Brooks was Green Bay's leading receiver and made his first Pro Bowl appearance.

go and Detroit up 24-21, Green Bay had the ball on the Lions' 40-yard line. Suddenly, Favre spotted Sharpe all alone in the end zone. Moving to his right, Favre threw a dangerous pass across his body at least 60 yards in the air. Sharpe grabbed it for the winning score.

Even though the Packers lost 27-17 to the Dallas Cowboys the following week, most Green Bay fans believed that the team's luck was finally changing. A third straight winning season in 1994 and another Wild Card playoff win against the Lions convinced even more people. However, there was one sad note when Sterling Sharpe, on his way to another record-breaking year, suffered a spinal injury that has put a hold on his career. Losing Sharpe was a blow to the Green Bay offense, but a new crew of wide receivers including Robert Brooks, Charles Jordan and Mark Ingram have helped to keep the Green Bay passing attack among the best in the league.

That passing attack moved to center stage in 1995, with Brett Favre establishing himself as the league's top quarterback and Most Valuable Player. Before the season, coach Holmgren had told reporters, "Brett Favre is the key. Our football team will almost automatically take the next step with him." Favre took giant steps in 1995, and so did the Packers. Favre topped the NFL with 359 completions for 4,413 yards and 38 touchdowns, to go along with only 13 interceptions. His passing also opened up the Green Bay running game, and Edgar Bennett became the team's first 1000-yard rusher since Terdell Middleton in 1978. With their balanced attack, the Packers won six of their last seven games to finish at 11-5 and charge into the playoffs.

Green Bay fans got into the act, too. Packers receivers, after crossing the end zone, would often hurl themselves into the

Tight end Mark Chmura caught many passes in heavy traffic.

Brett Favre was the NFL's Most Valuable Player in 1995.

Reggie White is the all-time NFL leader in sacks.   31

Ron Cox began his second season with the Packers after previously starring for Chicago.

stands to share the joyous moment with the crowd, many of whom had painted themselves green and gold.

Following playoff victories against the Atlanta Falcons (37-20) and the defending Super Bowl champion San Francisco 49ers (27-17), the Packers found themselves in a situation that seemed both familiar and new—facing off against the Dallas Cowboys for the NFC title. The two teams had last met in a championship game in the "Ice Bowl" on New Year's Eve, 1967. This time, the contest was almost as exciting, but the ending turned out differently, as the Cowboys rallied for two fourth-quarter touchdowns to win 38-27.

Despite the loss, the joy has faded only slightly in Green Bay. With Brett Favre at the quarterback helm, there is good reason for the fans to be optimistic. As Packers general manager Ron Wolf noted, "I think Favre can take it a step further. He's doing things right now at a young age that a lot of people thought he couldn't do. There's a part of him that can raise his level even more."

Mike Holmgren has put together a powerful squad that would make even Curly Lambeau and Vince Lombardi proud. These Packers are certain to be warming up those chilly fall and winter afternoons in Lambeau Field for many years to come.